Not Above the Law

Richard MacAndrew

CAMBRIDGE
ALIS

CAMBRIDGE UNIVERSITY PRESS
Cambridge, New York, Melbourne, Madrid, Cape Town, Singapore,
São Paulo, Delhi, Dubai, Tokyo

Cambridge University Press
The Edinburgh Building, Cambridge CB2 8RU, UK

www.cambridge.org
Information on this title: www.cambridge.org/9780521140966

First published 2010

Richard MacAndrew has asserted his right to be identified as the Author of the Work in
accordance with the Copyright, Designs and Patents Act 1988.

Printed in China by Sheck Wah Tong Printing Press Limited

Typeset by Aptara Inc.
Map artwork by Malcolm Barnes

A catalogue record for this publication is available from the British Library.

ISBN 978-0-521-14096-6 Paperback
ISBN 978-0-521-15768-1 Paperback plus 2 audio CDS

No character in this work is based on any person living or dead.
Any resemblance to an actual person or situation is purely coincidental.

With thanks to Ashley Blooms florists, Caversham.

Contents

Characters

George Keegan: a lawyer in Dublin, Ireland
Michael Sullivan: George's friend and a lawyer
Orla Quinn: George's girlfriend, also a lawyer
Sean Murphy: a police inspector
Tara Lynch: a police sergeant
Geraldine Keane: a believer in animal rights
Fergal McBride: a flower seller

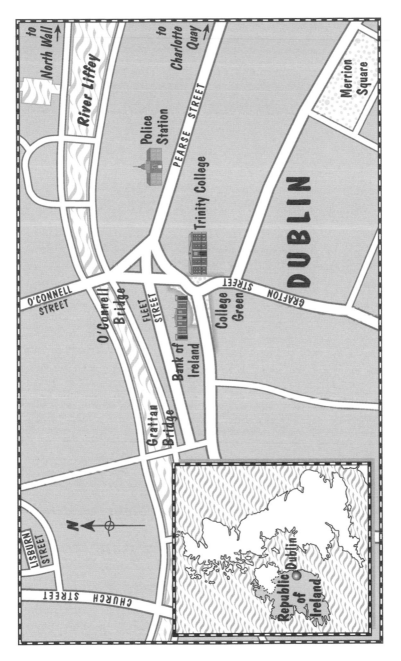

to North Wall

River Liffey

to Charlotte Quay

Police Station

PEARSE STREET

Trinity College

Merrion Square

DUBLIN

O'CONNELL STREET

O'Connell Bridge

FLEET STREET

Bank of Ireland

College Green

GRAFTON STREET

Grattan Bridge

N

LISBURN STREET

CHURCH STREET

Republic of Ireland

Dublin

Chapter 1 *Thick dark blood – and lots of it*

George Keegan opened his eyes. His head hurt. His mouth was dry and tasted strange. At first he had no idea where he was. He turned his head. It was 7 am. There was a clock on the small table beside the bed. His clock. His bed. His bedroom. He was at home. His head continued to hurt. He closed his eyes. Then suddenly he opened them again. OK, he was in his flat, in his own bed, but he felt terrible. Why? What had happened last night?

George lay on his back, looking up. He tried to remember where he had been, or who he had been with. He thought hard – but he had no idea. A party maybe? A night out with friends? He remembered going to work the day before, but that was all. Slowly he began to realise that his hand felt wet. In fact, the bed felt wet. Not wet with water, but something thicker. He took his hand out from under the sheet and looked at it. 'My God!' he shouted. It was blood, thick dark blood – and lots of it!

George sat straight up and threw back the sheet. What had happened? He was still fully dressed – dark blue trousers, pink shirt, socks and shoes – but there was blood everywhere! George jumped out of bed and immediately started pulling his clothes off. As he did so, he checked his body. Where had the blood come from? Had he fallen? Or cut himself? He seemed OK – except for the headache.

Thirty seconds later George stood, with no clothes on, in front of the bedroom mirror, looking at himself. He was tall and well built, with wild red hair. There were no cuts on his body, so it wasn't his own blood. But whose blood was it? There was so much of it. It wasn't just on his clothes and his sheets. There was some on the carpet, too. Was it only in the bedroom?

Quickly George made a tour of his flat. It wasn't big – a bedroom, a sitting room, a bathroom and a kitchen. The bathroom was clean, but there was blood in all the other rooms. In the kitchen there was blood on the floor, on the table and down the front of the cupboards. In the sitting room it was on the carpet and there was a little on the sofa. The bedroom was the worst.

'My God!' George said again, his hands shaking, as he stood in his bedroom looking round. 'Whose blood is this? What's happened?' He looked down at the blood on his hands.

'First things first,' he thought to himself. 'I've got to get clean. I've just got to get clean.' He went back to the bathroom and got in the shower. Ten minutes later he felt a bit better. Eight minutes of hot shower, soap and shampoo, then two minutes of ice-cold water. His body began to feel more normal, but his hands wouldn't stop shaking. He dried himself and put on clean clothes – black jeans, a green Ireland rugby shirt and trainers.

What should he do next? 'You should always wash blood off quickly and always use cold water,' George's mother used to say. 'Always wash blood off quickly.' He knew he wasn't thinking straight, but he couldn't help it. He didn't know what to think. He couldn't think! He put his bloody clothes and sheets in the washing machine together.

'Blood,' he said to himself. 'Cold wash. Cold water to wash off blood. Thanks Mum.'

He started the machine.

George's mouth was dry. His head still hurt. It hurt badly. He needed aspirin. And a drink. He made some tea, then found some aspirin and took two. He sat at the kitchen table and looked at his hands. He looked at them hard until they slowly stopped shaking. Then he began to think. What should he do? Call the police? Probably – but not just yet. Not right now. He needed to know more first, more about what had happened.

George started searching for his diary. It was on the table in the sitting room. Quickly he opened it at yesterday's date. There it was. *Thursday 17th March – 7.30 pm, CSI drinks, O'Gara's.* That was where he had been! O'Gara's was a bar near Grafton Street, Dublin's main shopping street. 'CSI drinks' meant he had had drinks with the 'Church Street Irregulars'. George was a lawyer. He shared offices in a building with several other lawyers. As a joke, they called themselves the Church Street Irregulars. Their offices were in Church Street and, like all lawyers, they worked very irregular hours – sometimes starting very early in the morning, sometimes finishing very late at night.

Bits and pieces of the evening came back to him. Although it was only a Thursday night, O'Gara's had been full. He remembered arriving at the bar with Frank Brady, whose office was next door to his. Michael Sullivan was already at the bar when they arrived. He was also a lawyer and George's friend. Had Orla been there? Or had she come later? He couldn't remember. His phone was next to his diary. He picked it up and called Orla's number. There was

8

no reply. The call went straight through to the answerphone. He spoke into it.

'Hi, Orla. It's George. I really need to talk to you about last night, about what happened. Call me quickly – as soon as you get this. Love you.'

George looked at the phone in his hand and then called another number.

'Michael Sullivan speaking.'

'Hi, Michael. It's George here. I'm sorry it's so early.'

'Hello there, George.' replied Michael. 'That's OK. I've been up for some time. How are you doing?'

'Not so bad,' answered George. 'Listen. I need to get a couple of things straight about last night.'

There was a laugh at the other end of the phone.

'Too much Guinness, George?' asked Michael, laughing again.

'Come on, Michael. You know I never drink much. But seriously, I was at O'Gara's last night, wasn't I?'

'Yes,' answered Michael, surprise in his voice. 'Don't you remember?'

'Well, not very clearly, actually.'

'Yes, you were there,' repeated Michael. He sounded more serious now. 'And Frank and Paul and quite a few others were there too. And Orla came along later. And then you left with Orla at about 11 o'clock.'

'Right,' said George.

He said nothing for a moment, asking himself where Orla was and why she wasn't answering her phone. Asking himself where the blood came from and whose blood it was. Not Orla's. It couldn't be Orla's. He couldn't even begin to think that! He heard Michael ask a question, but he wasn't really listening.

'I'm sorry, Michael, what did you say?'

'I asked, "Are you going out with Orla?" ' replied Michael.

George was going out with her, but they hadn't told anyone yet. It was only a couple of months since Orla had moved into the same building as George and joined the Church Street Irregulars. She didn't want everyone in the offices talking about her. But Michael had clearly put two and two together and got the right answer.

'Well, yes, I am going out with her actually,' said George. 'And even though it's still early days, it seems quite serious. But we don't want everyone talking about it. OK? It's a secret for the moment.'

'OK,' said Michael. 'No problem.'

Neither of them spoke for a few seconds.

Then Michael said, 'You sound a bit strange this morning, George. Is everything OK?'

'Fine, fine,' said George. 'Look I've got to go. I've got some cleaning to do. Don't worry about me. Everything's fine.'

But, as he turned off his phone and put it back on the table, George knew that everything was far from fine.

Chapter 2 *A crime of hate or madness*

Inspector Sean Murphy of the Dublin police was at his desk in the Pearse Street police station when the phone rang. It was 7.30 in the morning. He put down his first coffee of the day and picked up the phone.

'Murphy,' he said.

It was Fiona Whelan, his boss.

'Sean,' said Whelan. 'Get over to Grattan Bridge. Northside. They're pulling a body out of the water.'

'I'm on my way,' said Murphy. He quickly finished his coffee, took his jacket off the back of his chair and left the office. Outside it was cloudy. There was the smell of Irish rain in the air. It wasn't actually raining now, so Murphy decided to walk to the bridge. It wasn't far, but even at that time in the morning the Dublin traffic was bad.

Within a few minutes, he was walking beside the River Liffey. The dirty brown waters cut the city in two. On Murphy's right, across the water, was the north of the city – the 'Northside'. This was once an area where the poor and working class lived. Today, many people think of it as the 'real' Dublin. On his left was the 'Southside', where Dublin's rich and important people had made their homes. Here there were pretty squares, wide shopping streets and the beautiful 18th-century buildings of Trinity College.

Soon Murphy passed The Clarence hotel, owned by the rock band U2. Then he turned right across Grattan Bridge towards the Northside. There was a group of people standing near two police cars and a white police van. Behind the police van were some TV cameras and a few journalists. As he reached the group near the cars, a face he knew well turned towards him but did not smile.

'Good morning, sir.' It was Sergeant Tara Lynch. Murphy was pleased to see her. He and Lynch had worked on many cases together and liked each other.

'Morning, Sergeant,' he replied. 'What do we know?'

They pushed their way through to the front of the group. Murphy looked down at the lifeless body of a young woman lying by the side of the road. Her long brown hair was wet. Some of it lay across her face. Her short red party dress had been cut in many places. Her face had clearly been pretty, but in death it was empty of life and light. A man and a woman in white clothes – the forensics team – were looking at the body and making notes.

'It's a young woman. In her twenties probably,' began Lynch. 'We pulled her out about forty minutes ago. A man walking his dog saw the body and called us.'

Murphy did not ask questions. He knew that Lynch would tell him everything of importance.

'The doctor has had a look at her,' continued Lynch, 'and forensics will take the body away when you've seen it. The doctor put the time of death as late last night, or early this morning, between midnight and 2 am. She may be able to tell you more later. But it's clearly murder. The killer used a knife. And not just once. The woman died when the knife went through her heart.'

Murphy got down to look at the body. Through the holes in the dress he could see some of the cuts to the woman's chest and stomach. He counted nine or ten, but he could see that there must be more. 'A crime of hate or madness,' he thought to himself. He looked at the forensics team and nodded to them.

'OK,' he said. 'Take her away. Ring me when you have any more information.'

He stood up again and looked at Lynch.

'Do we know who she is?' he asked.

'This was on her wrist,' said Lynch, holding up a plastic bag. There was a circle of metal inside it. 'It's an "ICE" bracelet – In Case of Emergency. The name on it is Orla Quinn. It seems she had an unusual blood group. It's also got her doctor's name and number on it. I was just going to call the doctor when you arrived.'

'Do it now,' said Murphy. 'We need all the information we can get.'

Lynch moved along the road a little to find somewhere quieter and took out her phone. Murphy watched her. She was tall with short fair hair. When she walked into a room, heads turned to look at her. But she never made people think she was more important or better than them in any way. She was intelligent and thoughtful too. In fact, Murphy thought she was one of the best young police officers he had ever worked with. This might be one of the last cases they worked on together. It wouldn't be long before she was made an inspector.

After a couple of minutes Lynch closed her phone and came back.

'It's almost certainly Orla Quinn,' she said. 'The doctor knew her well and described her. She was 27. A lawyer. Her office is very close to here on Church Street.'

'She was clearly a clever young lady,' said Murphy.

He looked across the river towards the Southside, shaking his head at the unfairness of life – and death. He'd been a policeman for twenty years, a detective for fifteen, but some parts of the job always got to him.

Turning back to Lynch he asked, 'Have you got a home address for her?'

'A flat on Charlotte Quay over by the Grand Canal Docks,' replied Lynch. 'Dublin 4.'

The information told Murphy more about Orla Quinn. On both the Northside and the Southside of Dublin there had once been large docks. These were areas where large numbers of ships came and went. However, by the end of the 20th century, there were fewer and fewer ships. Old buildings in the dock areas were knocked down. New offices and flats were built. Forward-looking young men and women moved in. People like Orla Quinn. The area known as Dublin 4 was on the Southside – and one of the best areas on the Southside. Clearly Ms Quinn had both brains and money.

Murphy thought about this as he looked at Lynch. Neither of them spoke.

'Right,' said Murphy, coming to a decision. 'You send some officers over to Charlotte Quay. I want them to ask questions door-to-door round Orla Quinn's neighbours. When did they last see her? What was she like? Did she have any visitors? Who were they? The usual thing. Then you and I can go over to Church Street and ask around at some of the offices there. Lawyers work long hours. I'm sure some of them will be at their desks already. Let's hope somebody knows where she was last night.'

Chapter 3   *Face down in the water*

'First things first, my boy.' That's what George Keegan's grandfather had told George time and time again. 'Do things in the right order and everything will be OK.' He could almost hear his grandfather's voice.

George looked in his diary again. He had no meetings that morning. It wouldn't matter if he went in to work late. He called and left a message for his secretary, telling her he would be in after lunch. Then he looked round his flat and tried to decide what to do. Should he call the police? What could he say to them? 'I woke up this morning and there was blood all over my flat.' They'd think he was mad!

He looked round the living room, beginning to feel sick at seeing so much blood.

'No,' he thought. 'Not the police. Not yet. I'll clean first. Then try and find out what happened.'

He got a brush out of the kitchen cupboard and quickly filled a bowl with soapy water. He found some carpet cleaner that was probably five years old – he certainly didn't remember buying it. He started in the bedroom because that was the worst place. He worked fast – brushing, washing and cleaning. He felt sick and still had a bad headache.

While he cleaned, he tried to put together the pieces of the night before. Clearly everything had been normal when he and Orla had left O'Gara's. Michael hadn't told him about anything unusual. He should check his email and phone messages – but finish the cleaning first, he thought.

An hour and a half later, George put away the cleaning things and made himself a strong cup of coffee. His hands started to shake once more, as he tried again and again to remember the night before.

The flat hadn't been so clean for a long time. Except for some small dark areas on the bedroom carpet that were still wet, it was impossible to tell that anything had happened.

George put his coffee down shakily on the desk in his sitting room and turned on his computer. While he was waiting for it to start up, he picked up his phone and checked his messages. Nothing. He tried Orla's phone but it went straight through to the answerphone again. He didn't leave another message. He opened up his email. No new messages. He sent an email to Orla.

From: George Keegan
To: Orla Quinn
Subject: Last night

Please call me as soon as possible.

Love,

George

He tried his work email too – there was just a chance something was there – but no, nothing. He put his head in his hands. What terrible thing had happened? Had he done something awful? He had to know.

George sat there for a long time, thinking, drinking coffee, trying to decide what to do. His headache was really bad and he was still finding it difficult to think straight. He stood up and put on the television, turning immediately to the 24-hour news. As he watched, he walked up and down the room. It felt better if he kept moving. He didn't want to sit down. A journalist appeared on the TV in the middle of the countryside, walking beside a long low building.

'At three o'clock this morning five people broke into this building, where about 900 mink were kept,' she said. 'They freed all the animals and allowed them to escape into the countryside around the farm. Video cameras inside the building filmed the people breaking in. However, because the people were wearing hats, and scarves over their faces, police are not able to say who they were.'

George stopped walking around and began to watch. A couple of years ago, he had helped the police send some people like this to prison. What was their name? Oh yes, 'FLAIR'. Free Life for Animals in Ireland. They were an animal rights group who wanted all animals to be free, not kept in farms and zoos. But that time they hadn't just freed the animals – they had burned down the farmer's house as well.

The journalist was speaking again. 'An animal rights group calling itself FLAIR has told the police that this was their work. FLAIR say they will free more animals over the next few months. The animals kept here were mink. They were farmed for their skins, which would later be made into expensive coats. There are 140,000 mink on six farms in Ireland and police will now be watching the other farms carefully.'

The people who had burned down the farmer's house had been angry with George. When the police took them away, they had shouted at him. They had also pulled their fingers across their throats as if they were going to kill him. George hadn't been too worried. People were often angry when they got sent to prison. But they soon discovered there were more important things to think about. Living with other prisoners, for example, was never easy.

Now the journalist was talking to the farmer. The farmer was explaining how the escaped mink would destroy the countryside and kill other animals. George stopped listening, but then the next news story caught his interest.

'Early this morning police pulled the body of a young woman from the River Liffey, near Grattan Bridge. The body had been in the water for a few hours. It was first seen by a man walking his dog.'

George's hand went to his mouth and he sat down quickly. The TV showed a group of police officers at the side of the river near the bridge. There was a boat on the river with two police officers in it. Then there were pictures of a journalist talking to a grey-haired man with a beard. The man with the beard was speaking.

'I was just taking the dog out for a walk. I always do that in the morning. Well, anyway, I saw something red in the water. I went closer and there she was. Just lying face down in the water in a red dress. Terrible it was. That poor girl.'

'A red dress,' thought George. 'Orla has a red dress. But it can't be her! What was she wearing last night?' He couldn't remember. He still couldn't remember very much at all.

The TV now showed a body under a blanket being put into the back of a white police van. A small piece of dress was showing. Dark red. Just like Orla's. But it couldn't be!

Just then there was a loud knocking at the door.

'Mr Keegan,' said a voice. 'Open up, please. Police. Come on, Mr Keegan. Open up. We know you're in there.'

Chapter 4 *The sweet smell of chloroform*

Murphy and Lynch stood outside the front door of George Keegan's flat, with two other police officers behind them. They waited. George's flat was also in an area that had once been part of the docks. Although this area was on the Northside, in a part of the city called North Wall, it was also a place where the young and well-paid were moving in.

Murphy knocked loudly on the door again.

'Come on, Keegan,' he shouted. 'This is your last chance. Open up.'

Just as he finished speaking, the door opened. Murphy and Lynch held up their police ID cards.

'Are you George Keegan?' Murphy asked.

'Yes.' George nodded. He had one hand on the door as if he wanted to keep the police out of his flat.

'I'm Inspector Murphy. And this is Sergeant Lynch. We'd like to ask you a few questions.'

'Yes?' George didn't move.

'We'd like to come in if that's OK,' said Murphy.

George looked over Murphy's shoulder at the other two police officers standing behind him.

'Why?' he asked.

For a moment no one spoke. Murphy looked at George.

'Because it will be easier than talking at the door,' he said. 'And because it will show me you have nothing to hide.'

At first it looked as if George was going to shut the door, but then he took his hand away and stepped back.

Murphy and Lynch walked into the sitting room followed by the two other officers. George came in behind them. Murphy looked quickly round the room. It was medium-sized, with a sofa, two armchairs and a TV. There were books along one wall, a desk by the window and a light-coloured carpet on the floor.

'You seem worried, Mr Keegan,' said Lynch.

'No, no, I'm fine,' replied George. He gave a weak smile. 'Late night yesterday. Bit of a headache this morning.'

'Take a seat,' Lynch said.

George sat in one of the armchairs. His eyes moved quickly from one thing to another.

'You don't mind if these officers have a look round, do you?' Lynch asked. She was asking the questions, but Murphy was watching George carefully. To Murphy's eyes, Keegan looked like a man in trouble – and Murphy knew what to look for.

'Yes,' said George hurriedly, then changed his mind. 'I mean no. No, go on. Look round, if you want to.'

Murphy looked at the two officers and nodded. They left the room, putting on plastic gloves as they went.

'Where were you last night?' asked Lynch.

'O'Gara's bar,' replied George. 'With friends.'

'What time did you leave?'

'About eleven o'clock.'

'Did you leave alone?' asked Lynch.

'No. I was with my girlfriend, Orla Quinn.'

'Where did you go then?' asked Lynch.

'Sir!' A voice called from one of the other rooms. 'In the bedroom. Come and look at this.'

Murphy left the room. Lynch and George sat without speaking. They could hear Murphy talking quietly with the officer. Then the inspector went to the kitchen. There was more quiet talking. Then he appeared again in the sitting room. He had also put on some plastic gloves. In his right hand was a blue handkerchief. He held it towards Lynch.

'Smell that,' he said, 'but don't get too close.'

Lynch moved her nose a little closer, then moved back.

Murphy looked at George.

'Do you know what this smells of?' he asked George.

George said nothing.

'The sweet smell of chloroform,' said Murphy. 'I'm sure you know what that is. If I put some more chloroform on this handkerchief and hold it over your nose, you'll be asleep in about twenty seconds. Less, maybe.'

The two officers had come into the room behind Murphy. One started searching the room, the other was holding open a plastic bag. Murphy dropped the chloroformed handkerchief into the bag.

'Why was that at the back of one of your kitchen cupboards?' asked Murphy.

'I've never seen it before,' said George. He moved uncomfortably on the chair, looking from the handkerchief to Murphy's face and back again. 'I have no idea how it got there. I've certainly never bought any chloroform.'

Murphy looked at George.

'What are those dark areas on the carpet in your bedroom?' he asked.

George moved uncomfortably again. He was about to say something. But at that moment one of the officers spoke.

'Got something!' he said. He had his hands down the back of the sofa. He stood up and pulled his hands up from under the seat. In one gloved hand he held a piece of dark red material, in the other a long kitchen knife.

For a full minute no one spoke. Everyone looked at George. An awful look crossed his face. Several times he started to say something, but stopped himself each time. Finally he looked down at the floor, shaking his head slowly from side to side.

Murphy turned to the officer by the sofa.

'Put everything in bags,' he said. 'Call forensics. Wait until they come. Give them everything. Then you can go.'

The two officers left the room.

Murphy looked at Lynch and together they sat down opposite George. Murphy sat on the sofa, Lynch in the other armchair.

'You didn't answer me earlier,' said Lynch. 'Where did you go when you left O'Gara's?'

George's head came up again. He sat up straighter.

'Tell me something,' he looked from Murphy to Lynch and back again. 'The body that you found in the Liffey this morning – was that Orla Quinn?'

'It seems very probable,' replied Murphy.

'And was she murdered?'

'Yes,' said Murphy.

'Oh my God!' said George. His hand went up to his mouth. 'Oh no! Oh no!'

His body moved backwards and forwards on the chair. A strange look came into his eyes. His face looked different – sad, hurt or lost maybe. 'Or is he just acting?' Murphy asked himself.

George stopped moving.

'With a knife?' he asked.

'Mr Keegan,' began Lynch, 'Remember that you don't have to…'

'Yes, yes,' said George, waving his hand at them almost impatiently. 'I know all that.' He stood up. Quickly Murphy and Lynch stood up too. They didn't want him to escape.

'It's OK,' said George, waving a hand at them again. 'I'm not going anywhere. Just give me a moment to think.'

He walked over to the window and looked out. Murphy and Lynch watched his back, but they didn't sit down. Finally George turned round.

'I'm a lawyer,' he said.

'We know,' replied Lynch.

'I should refuse to say anything. What I ought to do is get another lawyer here to give me advice,' said George.

Murphy and Lynch said nothing. Keegan could call a lawyer if he wanted to. They couldn't stop him. But they might find out more if he was alone.

'But I'm not going to call a lawyer,' continued George. 'It may be stupid, but I'm not going to do that. I'm going to tell you the truth, the complete truth, and hope that you believe me.'

George came back and sat down heavily in the armchair. His face was white. He looked ill. Murphy realised it would be a mistake to say anything. If he or Lynch started speaking, Keegan might stop. They didn't want that. They wanted to hear everything he had to say.

'I was at O'Gara's last night,' George went on. 'I remember that. I remember arriving there, but that's the last thing I remember. A friend of mine told me that I left at about 11 o'clock, with Orla Quinn, but I remember nothing else until this morning. I woke up in my bed with all my clothes on. There was blood on my clothes, on my sheets, on the carpet in the bedroom, in here and in the kitchen. Blood everywhere. It was terrible. I have no idea how it got here. I really don't. You have to believe me.'

He stopped for a moment and looked away to the side.

Then he said, 'Orla and I started going out together three weeks ago. She was the best thing that had ever happened to me. I wouldn't . . . I couldn't kill anyone. Certainly not her.'

He looked down at the floor again. The 'lost' look returned to his eyes.

'Sadness or clever acting?' Murphy asked himself again.

Murphy stood up. So did Lynch.

'Thank you, Mr Keegan,' said Murphy quietly. He had heard a lot of stories in his time as a police officer. Some were true, most weren't. It would take something special to make him believe this one.

'That's really not good enough,' he said. 'It's a pity you can't remember more, because what you've just told us is difficult to believe. I'm afraid we'll have to take you down to the police station and ask you some more questions.'

Chapter 5 *The smallest feeling of hope*

George Keegan sat, on his own, in a small windowless room in the Pearse Street police station. It was four o'clock on Friday afternoon. He was tired. There were four chairs and a table and no other furniture. There was a cassette recorder on the table and an empty teacup.

Murphy and Lynch had asked him questions all morning and most of the afternoon. They had started with yesterday morning and asked about everything he'd done before he'd arrived at O'Gara's. That was the easy part. Then they started asking questions about this morning. That was not so easy. Why had he washed the sheets? Why had he washed his clothes? Why had he cleaned the flat so carefully? If there was so much blood, why hadn't he called the police immediately? He was an intelligent man. Something terrible had happened – clearly a crime. But George kept to the truth. His truth.

Then they asked him about his past. Where had he studied law? How many girlfriends had he had? What were their names and addresses? Had he ever hit them or hurt them? How long had he been a lawyer? How long had he had an office in Church Street?

At midday Murphy and Lynch stopped for lunch. An hour later they came back and asked all the same questions again. And then a third time.

Part of George was worried, very worried, that they did not – or would not – believe him. Or, worse, he was worried that he really had killed Orla and thrown her body in the Liffey, but for some reason could not remember anything about it. Yet another part of him, the lawyer, was interested in how the police asked him questions. He knew they usually worked in twos – one hard, the other soft. One would ask the difficult questions and maybe get angry. The other would be kinder and say things like 'Come on. You know you did it. Just tell us. You'll feel much better afterwards.' It was interesting to watch Murphy and Lynch work together. Lynch was hard, Murphy soft. George had expected it to be the other way round. But it was Lynch who never smiled, who called him a murderer, and who said she didn't believe a word he was saying. Murphy spoke to him quietly. He put a hand on his arm from time to time. And he more or less said that if Keegan told them everything now, he wouldn't go to prison for so long.

Murphy sat in his windowless room thinking about all of this.

At around four thirty, the door opened and Murphy and Lynch came back into the room. They sat down on the chairs across the table from George. George looked from one to the other, hoping that he wouldn't have to answer the same questions for a fourth time.

Murphy put his arms on the table and looked at George.

'Mr Keegan,' he began, 'let's say you're telling the truth. I'm not saying that you really are telling the truth, but for now let's say you are. As a police officer, I have to look at everything that might be possible. And it might just be possible that you are telling the truth.'

George said nothing. He just waited to hear more.

'In which case,' continued Murphy, 'if you didn't kill Ms Quinn, who did?' Murphy's eyes opened wider as he asked the question. 'It could be someone who really didn't like her and wanted her dead. I've got officers looking at that idea. However, the murderer could also be someone who doesn't like you, and wants to make real problems for you. Have you thought about who might want to do that?'

For the first time since arriving at the police station, George allowed himself the smallest feeling of hope. The police might actually believe him. They were asking him the question he had already asked himself many times that afternoon.

George sat forward and looked at Murphy.

'Thank you,' he said. 'Thank you for at least trying to believe me – for a time anyway.' He looked at Lynch and then back at Murphy. 'Who would want to do this to me?' George asked. 'Well, I'm a lawyer, so quite a few people are in prison because of me. I'm sure none of them are too happy about being there. However, I can only think of a couple of people who might really want to do something like this.'

Lynch took out a pen while George was speaking.

'There's a man called Patrick Duffy,' said George. 'He robbed a bank on O'Connell Street about three or four years ago. He said again and again that he didn't do it but ... Well, he got ten years in prison. He was really angry about it.'

Lynch was writing in her notebook.

'And then the news this morning made me think of the other person. A woman called Geraldine Keane. She belonged – in fact she probably still belongs – to a group of people who call themselves FLAIR.'

Lynch and Murphy looked at each other, then back at George.

'There was Keane and her boyfriend. They were known as "The FLAIR Two." His name was Niall Campbell. They freed some animals from a farm near Cork. Unfortunately they set fire to the farmer's house as well and it burned down to the ground. When the police were taking them away, they shouted that they would kill me when they got out. And Keane pulled a finger across her throat like this.' George showed the police what he meant.

'They were certainly serious about it at the time,' said George. 'I was happy that there were police officers with them and that I was on the other side of the room. Campbell died in prison a year later. But Keane must be out by now. I don't know if she still wants to kill me. Or whether she would kill someone else to make trouble for me. But anyone who burns down someone's house. Well ...' George stopped speaking as he searched for the right words '... I'd say it could also be her.'

George looked down at his hands and then back up at Lynch and then at Murphy.

'Thank you, Mr Keegan,' said Murphy. 'We'll talk to these two people and see what they have to say for themselves. But don't get your hopes up. Like I said, we're just being careful, looking at the big picture.'

Murphy and Lynch stood up.

Lynch spoke. 'There's a man called Michael Sullivan outside. He says he's a lawyer and a friend of yours. He wants to have a talk with you, and try and get you out of here. I'm happy for him to talk to you, but we're keeping you here until tomorrow morning at least.'

George didn't know how Michael had found out he was at the police station, but it would be good to see a friendly face. And good to have some help!

Chapter 6   *An angry young woman*

Back in his office, Sean Murphy looked across his desk at Tara Lynch.

'Do we still think he did it?' he asked.

'He's our best hope at the moment,' replied Lynch.

Murphy coughed and looked out of the window. The first finger of his right hand was drawing circles on the desk in front of him.

'But I'm not a hundred percent sure,' added Lynch. 'I think we should check out the names he gave us.'

Murphy's hand stopped moving.

'Yes,' he said, 'we should.' He looked at Lynch. 'If he really did it,' he continued, 'you would expect him to have a better story than "I can't remember," wouldn't you?'

'True,' agreed Lynch.

'Anyway,' Murphy stood up, 'that lawyer will want to get him out of here tomorrow morning. He'll say that Keegan's a lawyer, has never been in trouble before, and will come back and answer more questions any time we want. We could try and keep Keegan for longer, but I don't think it's worth it at the moment.'

'I agree,' said Lynch.

'OK. Get someone to check on Patrick Duffy,' continued Murphy. 'I've known Duffy a long time and I don't see him as a killer. For him, crime is a profession, and going to prison is just something that happens when you have a bit of bad luck. It's possible that he didn't actually rob the

29

bank on O'Connell Street. But I'm sure there are a lot of other crimes that we don't know about – crimes that should be against his name on the police computer. I'd be very surprised if he's behind all this.'

Lynch wrote in her notebook.

'What about Geraldine Keane? she asked.

'We'll go and talk to her,' he said. 'I remember the FLAIR case and I remember Geraldine Keane. She was an angry young woman. Angry and a bit wild. It could easily be her. We'll go and see what she has to say.'

*   *   *

Forty-five minutes later, Murphy was standing outside a small house on Lisburn Street in the Northside. Lynch was beside him. Weak sunshine was trying to break through the clouds. Murphy knocked on the rather dirty front door.

'Who is it?' a voice asked.

'Police, Ms Keane,' replied Murphy. 'Open up, please.'

The door was opened quickly by a woman in her late twenties. She was medium height with long dark hair tied up at the back of her head. She was wearing a large blue wool sweater and jeans. She looked tired and cross, her lips pressed together. She kept one hand on the door, ready to close it.

'Not again,' she said angrily. 'I've answered all your questions already. I wasn't in Kildare last night. I wasn't anywhere near the mink farm. I was at my boyfriend's. You've got his name and address. I got back here at about ten this morning. I've been answering questions ever since. So go away and leave me alone.'

She started to close the door.

Murphy put up a hand and pushed against the door, stopping her from closing it.

'Not so fast,' he said. 'We've got some different questions.'

Murphy and Keane looked at each other. Keane was still trying to close the door. Then she stopped.

'OK,' she said. 'Come in then. But make it quick.'

'I'll take as much time as I want,' thought Murphy. But he said thank you.

Murphy and Lynch followed Keane into the small living room. There were magazines and CDs lying on the floor, dirty cups and plates on the table, books everywhere.

Murphy looked around, but there was nowhere to sit down. Every chair had something on it – clothes, more books, an old newspaper. He stayed standing. He looked at Lynch and nodded at her. He wanted her to ask the questions to begin with, so he could watch Keane.

'What time did you get to your boyfriend's last night?' asked Lynch.

'Sometime after midnight,' replied Keane.

'That's late to visit someone,' said Lynch.

'He works late. He doesn't get home till two usually.'

'Where were you before that?'

'Before that?' There was surprise in Keane's voice. 'I thought the mink were freed in the early hours of the morning.'

'Like I said, we have some different questions,' said Murphy.

'So where were you?' Lynch repeated the question.

'Here,' replied Keane.

'Alone?' asked Lynch.

'Yes.' Keane looked from one to the other. 'Is that a problem?' she asked.

Neither Murphy nor Lynch spoke.

Murphy was looking at Keane. When she had opened the door earlier, she had used her left hand. Her right hand had stayed behind the door and he hadn't been able to see it. Looking at it now, he could see there was a white bandage round it. He nodded at her hand.

'Why have you got a bandage on your hand?' he asked. 'Have you cut yourself?'

'No. It's the new fashion,' replied Keane, with a hard look in her eyes. 'Of course I cut myself.'

'How did you do that?' asked Lynch.

'With a knife. What do you think?'

'When?'

'Yesterday evening, if you must know,' replied Keane.

'How?' asked Lynch.

'What's this all about? Why the sudden interest in my hand?'

'Do you know George Keegan?' asked Murphy.

'That snake!' Keane almost shouted. 'I spent three and a half years in prison because of him.'

'No,' said Lynch quietly. 'You spent three and a half years in prison because you burned down a house.'

'Like I said, he's a snake,' repeated Keane. 'I've always thought so.' She started walking up and down, picking up things and putting them down again.

'Have you seen him lately?' asked Lynch. 'Or had anything to do with him?'

Keane stopped moving and looked at the officers.

'Why would I want anything to do with him?' she asked.

'You said things to him when you were sent to prison,' said Lynch. 'You said you'd kill him.'

'I didn't do that,' said Keane. 'You've got the wrong person. The people who broke in did a good job – but it wasn't me. I wasn't anywhere near the place.'

'Do you know who the police lawyer was going to be for the break-in?' asked Lynch.

Keane said nothing.

'Well?' asked Lynch again.

'Someone told me it was going to be Michael Sullivan,' said Keane.

'Well, they were wrong,' said Lynch. 'It was a woman called Orla Quinn.'

'Oh!' Keane's eyes opened wide.

'You look surprised,' said Lynch.

'No,' said Keane quickly, as a strange look passed across her face.

Lynch looked quickly at Murphy, then asked, 'Do you know Orla Quinn?'

'No,' replied Keane.

'Quinn was George Keegan's girlfriend.'

Keane looked questioningly at Lynch.

'Was?' she asked.

'Yes. Someone murdered her late last night or early this morning.'

Keane's eyes opened wide but she did not look away.

'You can't think that I had anything to do with that,' she said.

'Didn't you?' asked Murphy, watching her carefully and speaking for the first time.

'Of course not. I don't know her.'

'When we were at your house you said you'd always thought George Keegan was a snake. Why "always"?' asked Murphy.

Keane watched Murphy carefully.

'After I left school,' she began, 'I decided to become a lawyer. I studied law for two years at Trinity College. It was a four-year course. I left halfway through.'

She sat back in her chair, still looking at Murphy.

'George Keegan was there at the same time,' she continued. 'Not in my year. He was a couple of years ahead of me. He didn't know me, but I knew him. I knew who he was. Everyone did. He was very pleased with himself in those days. He probably still is.'

'Why did you give up the course?' asked Lynch.

'I became more interested in rights for animals and less interested in the rights of people,' replied Keane. 'If people looked after animals better, they might look after each other better.'

Murphy was still watching Keane closely and she began to seem uncomfortable. She looked down at her hands on the table.

'How many other lawyers do you know in Dublin from your time at Trinity College?' asked Murphy.

Keane looked up quickly.

'What kind of question is that?' she asked.

'A fairly easy one, I should think,' replied Murphy.

'Well, I've had enough of your questions,' said Keane. 'I want a lawyer now.'

Murphy and Lynch looked at each other.

Just then there was a knock at the door. A woman police officer came in and gave Murphy a piece of paper. He read it and passed it to Lynch. She read it and passed it back.

'Just a moment,' said Murphy. He and Lynch stood up and went to the door. Standing there, they had a quick whispered conversation. Only a few words reached Keane. 'Lawyer ... say nothing ... not worth the trouble ... knife ... blood ... let her go ...'

Then Murphy looked at Keane.

'OK, Ms Keane,' he said. 'You're free to go.'

Surprised, Geraldine stood up and started towards the door.

Murphy put up a hand to stop her for a moment.

'However,' he said, 'you should know I'm a man who doesn't like unanswered questions.'

Keane looked at him.

'I'll be interested to find out who was at Trinity College when you were there. I'll also be interested to know if any of those people are working here in Dublin right now. If I have time, I might even talk to one or two of them.'

Keane's face darkened but she said nothing. She pushed between the two officers and opened the door.

Murphy smiled.

'Don't leave Dublin,' he said as she walked out of the door.

Lynch went back into the room to pick up her papers from the table.

'My uncle works at Trinity College,' she said. 'He's not in the School of Law, but I'm sure he'd be happy to ask people who are. Would you like me to give him a call?'

Chapter 8 *A useful thing to know*

At 10.30 on Saturday morning, George Keegan and Michael Sullivan stepped out of the Pearse Street police station. Crossing the road, they walked up towards the main entrance of Trinity College. 'Thanks Michael, for getting me out of there,' said George.

'You're very welcome,' replied Sullivan. 'It was the least I could do. Anyway, the police seemed happy to let you go – so long as you don't leave Dublin.'

They stopped outside Trinity College and looked across College Green at the interesting 18th-century Bank of Ireland building.

'Well, thanks again,' said George, putting a hand on Sullivan's shoulder. 'Now, don't let me take up more of your weekend. I've got a lot of thinking to do.' He took his hand away.

Sullivan looked closely at George. 'Are you sure, George?' he asked. 'I mean, I can stay around if you want, if you think it might help.'

'No, no,' said George. 'You go off and enjoy the rest of the weekend. I'm going to go home. I need to see if I can remember any more of what happened.'

They shook hands, then George watched Sullivan walk away and round the corner to where he had left his car. George walked on as far as O'Connell Bridge. He stopped there and looked down into the Liffey as it moved slowly past him out towards the sea. As he looked down, thoughts and questions crowded into his mind. 'Who had murdered Orla? Why had they done it? Did they want her dead or did they want him in prison? Or both?' He needed to know what had happened and why. He needed answers.

'If someone wants to make trouble for me,' thought George, 'then killing my girlfriend is a strange way to do it. I think someone wanted to kill Orla. And I just happened to be in the wrong place at the wrong time.'

George started walking along beside the river. 'So,' he said to himself, 'two important questions – who wanted to kill Orla? And why?'

As he walked, he thought. He went through everything he knew about Orla Quinn – her friends, her family, her work. She had never talked much about herself and he hadn't known her long. Still, he couldn't think of a reason why anyone would want her dead. Soon he found himself crossing the river and walking up Church Street, towards the building where his office was. Orla's office was on the floor above his. George entered the empty building and went up the stairs.

A few years before, George had been the lawyer for a man called Kieran O'Connor. Kieran's 'profession' was breaking into houses, and stealing anything that looked valuable. He had been in prison a few times. And he knew that if he got sent there again, it would be for a long time. George made sure he wasn't sent to prison. Kieran was a happy man. In fact, he was so happy that he offered to teach George all he knew about locks. George had been interested. He thought that it might be a useful thing to know one day. And that day was today.

Opening the door to Orla's office was easy.

Her office was on the second floor, looking out on the road. There were papers all over her desk and more on the floor under the window. However, George knew that Orla was actually very well organised. The papers on her desk were in small piles. Each pile of paper was carefully tied up with red tape. The papers in each pile were about something she was working on at the moment. The papers under the window were about things she hadn't started work on yet.

George looked through the piles on the desk first. He knew about some of them because Orla had told him about them. They were mainly to do with small crimes – a robbery, a fight outside a nightclub, dangerous driving. None of them looked serious enough to lead to her murder. George turned to the papers on the floor. Almost immediately a name jumped out at him – Free Life for Animals in Ireland. FLAIR again! He untied the pile and looked through the papers. They were about a break-in at the offices of a drug company eighteen months before. Some people had broken in, thinking that the company was using animals to test soap and shampoo. In fact, there were no animals there, but they had broken windows and destroyed machines anyway. A week later four people were caught. Geraldine Keane had been one of them.

George looked quickly through the notes. Had Orla read them? Possibly not. She hadn't said anything to him. She hadn't written anything on the notes either. Did Geraldine Keane know that Orla Quinn was working on this? Did Orla know about George's history with FLAIR? Probably not. It had all happened a long time before she moved into the building. Questions and more questions. Not enough answers.

George tied up the notes again with the red tape and put them back on the floor. Standing up, he thought there was one more place where he might find useful information – Orla's flat.

*   *   *

Half an hour later George Keegan opened the door of Orla Quinn's flat in Charlotte Quay. He locked it behind him. The flat was bigger than his – it had two bedrooms, not one. The living room was larger too, with big windows that looked over the old dock area. There was a walk-in clothes cupboard by the front door. George opened it and looked in, but there was nothing of interest inside. He moved into the living room. Outside each window was a window box full of flowers. George had helped put the window boxes there the weekend before. The room was comfortable. He liked it all – the furniture, the pictures, the colours – Orla had had great taste.

Suddenly, as he stood in her living room, he could smell Orla's favourite perfume. He remembered her intelligence, her lovely laugh, the softness of her touch – and then the awfulness of her death hit him. He felt a dark emptiness in his heart. He didn't know if he wanted to shout or scream or cry. He fought against his feelings, knowing that he couldn't stay too long in the flat. The police had probably been there already, but they might come back at any time.

Looking round, George saw a bowl of fresh fruit on the table, and then something strange in the waste paper basket near the sofa. As well as an old magazine and an empty plastic bottle, there were some flowers – half-dead and still in their paper from the shop. It was three or four days since he had last been in Orla's flat and the flowers hadn't been there then. There was a small envelope tied to the flowers. Maybe there was a card inside from the person who'd sent them.

George was just about to cross the room and pick up the flowers when he heard something. There was the sound of voices and a key being put in the lock of the front door. George looked round quickly. Where could he hide? Almost without thinking, he ran to the clothes cupboard, got inside, and pulled the door towards him. He didn't close it completely. He wanted to see who was coming in.

Seconds later he heard voices.

'OK. Let's see what we've got.' It was Inspector Murphy. A moment later Murphy and his sergeant walked past the clothes cupboard into the flat.

'It looks like a living room, a kitchen, a bathroom and two bedrooms,' replied Sergeant Lynch.

'Right,' said Murphy. 'You take care of the kitchen, I'll have a look in the living room. I know you sent some officers here yesterday, but I always like to have a look round myself.'

'Me too,' agreed Lynch. 'You never know. Something might seem quite unimportant when actually it's the key to everything.'

From his hiding place, George saw Murphy go into the living room and Lynch into the kitchen. This was his chance. Quickly he came out of the cupboard, opened the front door and ran for the stairs.

Chapter 9   *Half-dead flowers*

Tara Lynch was opening Orla Quinn's refrigerator when she heard the front door close. She ran out of the kitchen just as Sean Murphy appeared from the living room.

'What was that?' asked Murphy.

Lynch did not reply. She threw the front door open and ran for the stairs. Murphy pressed the button for the lift but it was at the top of the building. It slowly started to come down. Before the lift arrived, Lynch was back.

'I didn't see who it was,' she said. 'By the time I got to the bottom there was no one around.'

'Did you close the front door when we came in?' asked Murphy.

'I think so,' replied Lynch, 'but I can't be sure.'

'Oh well,' said Murphy. 'Maybe we just heard it closing by itself. Anyway, if there was someone here, there's nothing we can do about it now. Let's get on with the search.'

They returned to Orla Quinn's flat. This time, Tara Lynch made sure she closed the front door carefully behind them. Then she went back to the kitchen, and Murphy to the living room. Murphy always searched a room the same way. He started on the right and worked around the sides of the room. Then he worked through the middle of the room. On the right was a bookcase – mainly books about law, a few travel books and a large book of photos from different parts of the world. Murphy looked quickly through each book. Books were good places to hide pieces of paper – but he found nothing there.

Next to the bookcase was the TV. There were a few DVDs on top of the DVD player. He looked inside the boxes but there was nothing unusual.

Opposite the TV was an armchair. He pushed his hands down the back of the chair but found nothing. He turned the chair on its side and looked at the bottom. Again he found nothing.

Beside the sofa was a waste paper basket. There were some half-dead flowers in it, still in paper. And there was an envelope tied to the flowers. Murphy stood and looked for a moment. Then he took a pencil out of his pocket and used it to open the envelope. It was empty.

'Tara,' he called. In public and at the police station she was 'Sergeant Lynch', and she called him 'Sir'. When no one else was there, and because they were friends, she was 'Tara' and he was 'Sean'.

'What is it?' Tara Lynch came out of the kitchen with a cookery book in her hands.

'If I gave you some flowers, what would you do with them?' asked Murphy.

'I'd say thank you,' said Lynch, smiling. 'But, really, you're old enough to be my dad!'

Murphy smiled.

'And what would you do after thanking me, and making fun of me?' he asked.

'I'd put them in water,' replied Lynch.

'Right,' said Murphy, nodding towards the waste paper basket.

Lynch saw the dead flowers.

'Ah!' she said. 'I see what you mean. An unwanted present. Perhaps from an unwanted friend.' Lynch's voice made it quite clear that 'friend' was not what she meant. 'Unwelcome friend, perhaps,' she added.

Lynch reached down and picked the flowers carefully out of the basket, holding the paper with the very ends of her fingers. She looked at the flowers.

'Not cheap, these,' she said. 'Probably cost about €40.'

Then she looked down into the basket.

'There are some pieces of card down here, Sean,' she said, putting the flowers on the coffee table in front of the sofa. Murphy picked up the basket and carefully emptied out the pieces.

'It's the card that was in the envelope,' he said. There was writing on some of the pieces. Murphy got down on his knees next to the table. With his pencil and a key, being careful not to touch anything with his fingers, he started turning over some of the pieces and moving them round. Lynch got down next to him and helped. Within a few seconds they put it together.

It was good to see you again today.
When we get together,
I will complete your life. ♡

Murphy and Lynch read the message and then looked at each other.

'What does that say to you?' asked Murphy. Lynch did not reply immediately.

Then she said, 'I'm not sure. "I will complete your life" could mean two things. It could mean "I will make your life complete." You know, something like "Together we will make a great couple.'"

'Or?' asked Murphy.

'Or "complete" could mean "finish". So it could mean "I will end your life."'

Then she added thoughtfully, 'Since the message came with flowers and there's a heart, I'd probably choose the first meaning – we'd make a great couple.'

'And what about this?' asked Murphy. '"It was good to see you again today." Did they meet? Or did he, if it is a "he", just see her? Maybe he was watching her and she didn't know. Maybe he could see her but she couldn't see him. I mean, there's no name on the card.'

He looked at Lynch.

'I like your idea of the unwelcome friend,' he said.

Lynch shook herself a little. 'It's horrible,' she said. 'It makes me feel really uncomfortable.'

'Yes, I'm sure it does,' agreed Murphy, 'but we both know that it happens.' He read out the second sentence.

'"When we get together, I will complete your life,"' he said. 'There are strong feelings in those words.'

'Maybe dangerously strong,' added Lynch.

Murphy stood up.

'Give forensics a ring,' he said, 'and get them over here. If this person came to the flat, forensics may be able to tell us something about him.'

Lynch took her phone from her pocket.

'We'll finish the search here,' continued Murphy. 'Then we'll go round to the flower shop and see what they can tell us. The address is on the paper. It's not far away.'

Chapter 10 *Something important in the conversation*

George had run towards the stairs. As he started down them, he heard the front door of Orla's flat close noisily.

'Oh no!' he thought. 'Murphy and Lynch will hear that.' George ran faster down the stairs. He heard Orla's front door open, and then footsteps as someone started down behind him. He reached the ground floor, threw open the doors and ran out onto the road. George looked quickly left and right. To the left and across the road was a small street. He ran into it, then immediately turned right into another small street. There were small houses on one side of the road, and a new building development on the other side. No one had seen him, no one was following. There was a taxi parked at the side of the street. A dark-haired woman had just paid the driver. George ran to the taxi and looked in through the open window.

'Are you free?' he asked.

'Yes,' answered the driver.

George opened the back door.

'North Wall, please,' he said, climbing into the car.

Soon they were heading along Pearse Street, past the police station where he had spent Friday night. Twenty minutes later George was back in his own flat. He threw his keys on the table in the kitchen and made himself a cup of tea. He took his tea into the living room and sat in his

47

favourite armchair. Sitting, drinking his tea, George looked at the wall opposite and thought about the flowers in Orla's flat. Who had bought them? He certainly hadn't. He was sure she hadn't. Orla loved flowers. She often bought flowers for herself. When she got home, she always put them straight into water. She would never throw them into a waste paper basket. Except ... the only reason she might do that was if she didn't like the person who gave her the flowers. It was a pity the police had arrived so soon. He hadn't had time to see if there was a card in the envelope.

George put down his empty cup and tried to think of someone who would give Orla flowers, someone she didn't like. He couldn't.

Just then the phone rang.

'George. It's Michael. I'm just ringing to see how you are.'

'I'm fine,' replied George, standing up and looking out of the window as he spoke. 'Listen,' he continued. 'I went over to the office and had a look through Orla's papers.'

'Do you think you should be doing that?' asked Michael. 'I mean, this is a murder.'

'I know,' replied George. 'That's why I was looking. I want to find out who killed her. Anyway, there were some papers about a group called FLAIR – the animal rights people. Do you know anything about that?'

'Yes, I do,' replied Michael. 'In fact I was asked to work on it at first, but I decided I couldn't.'

'You couldn't. Why not?' asked George.

'It's a long story,' said Michael. 'Anyway, I asked Orla to do it. She was fairly new in town. I thought she might need the work. And I thought she might give me something in return later.'

'You don't know if she'd read the notes about FLAIR, do you?' asked George.

'Sorry. I can't help you there. She hadn't had them very long. I do know that.'

Neither of them spoke for a moment. Then George said, 'You see, I think the killer wanted her dead. And it was just useful for the killer that I happened to be there at the time.'

'Right,' said Michael. 'I mean, you'd only been going out with her for three weeks and you hadn't told anyone so ...' He stopped speaking.

'Right,' replied George. 'Anyway, after that I went round to her flat.'

'George,' said Michael seriously. 'You really shouldn't do things like that. If the police find out ...' Again, he didn't finish.

'I know, I know,' replied George, remembering very clearly the noise of the key in the lock as Murphy and Lynch had arrived. He remembered too how his heart had gone faster and his mouth had become dry. 'I should be more careful,' he continued. 'Anyway, I went round there and I found some dead flowers in the waste paper basket. They were still in their paper.'

There was a noise like a cough at the other end of the phone.

Then Michael said, 'I don't understand.'

'Neither do I,' replied George. 'Orla loved flowers.'

'You could see that from her window boxes,' agreed Michael.

'So why did she throw the flowers away?' asked George.

'No idea,' replied Michael. 'Look. Would you like me to come round? I can if you want – or are you OK?'

'No. No. I'm fine,' replied George. 'I'll give you a call tomorrow sometime.'

'OK,' said Michael. 'I'll speak to you then.'

George put the phone down and sat down again in the armchair. He sat there for a full minute, not moving, just thinking. His eyes were looking at the wall. In fact, at a picture of countryside near the west coast of Ireland. But he saw nothing. Something was worrying him, but he didn't know what. Something Michael had said. There had been something important in the conversation.

George knew that thinking more about it wouldn't help. He needed to think about something else. He picked up his cup and took it through to the kitchen. Then he went back to the sitting room. His diary was on the table. It was open. He looked at the picture again. There were flowers on the hillside. The diary. The picture. Dates. Flowers ... That was it!

He stood in the middle of the room, trying to tie down the thoughts that were flying around inside his head. He couldn't be right, could he? Had he really found out who the killer was?

He reached for the keys to his motorbike. This was a conversation he couldn't have on the phone. It had to be done in person.

Chapter 11 *Fergal's Flowers*

Inspector Sean Murphy pushed open the door of Fergal's Flowers and walked in. Tara Lynch came in behind him. A tall blonde girl was cutting the bottoms off some flowers and putting them in water. She looked up as Murphy introduced himself and showed her his police ID card.

'I'd like to ask you a few questions,' he explained.

The girl smiled.

'One moment, please,' she said. 'I'm just the shop assistant. I'll get the boss.'

As soon as he heard the girl speak, Murphy realised she was not Irish. Her English was good, but from the way she spoke Murphy thought she was probably from somewhere in Eastern Europe. There were a lot of young Eastern Europeans in Dublin. Some of them worked in hotels, restaurants, and bars – flower shops too, it seemed. It gave the city a nice international feeling.

The girl disappeared into the back of the shop and came out a moment later. She was followed by a short man wearing a light blue shirt and jeans. The man held out his hand to Murphy.

'Fergal McBride,' he said, shaking Murphy's hand. 'How can I help you?'

Murphy explained that they were trying to find out who had sent flowers to Orla Quinn.

'Well,' said McBride, reaching across and pulling down a large book. 'I can look in my order book. If we took the flowers round to Charlotte Quay, I should have the name and address of the person who made the order. When did you say it was?'

'Probably three or four days ago,' replied Murphy, thinking of the condition of the flowers.

Fergal McBride started looking through his order book. He turned back a few pages and stopped.

'Here it is,' he said. 'Wednesday 16th March. €45. And a name, an address and a credit card number.' He turned the book round so that Murphy and Lynch could look at it.

It read: Pat Higgins, 15 Fleet St, Dublin 2. There was a credit card number and a phone number. Lynch wrote down the information.

'Can you remember anything about the person who made the order?' asked Lynch.

McBride shook his head.

'We get forty or fifty people a day in here and maybe ten or twenty phone calls,' said McBride, 'sometimes more. That's my handwriting on the order but, to tell you the truth, I can't even remember if it was a man or a woman.'

Outside the shop Murphy gave the piece of paper to Lynch.

'Who lives in Fleet Street?' he asked.

'Sorry?' Lynch was surprised by the question.

'I asked, "Who lives in Fleet Street?"' said Murphy. 'I'll tell you. No one. It's just hotels and bars and restaurants. I'm almost certain no one actually lives there.'

'So ... what do you mean?' asked Lynch.

'I mean the person who made the order didn't give their real name and address. That's what I think anyway,' replied

Murphy. 'Try the phone number and see who answers,' he added.

Lynch took out her phone and tried the number. Twenty seconds later she put the phone back in her pocket.

'You were right,' she said. 'It's not a real number.'

'Well, the credit card number must be real,' said Murphy, getting into the car. 'So give the card company a call and find out what you can. Then we'll go and visit the person who really owns the card.'

Lynch took out her phone, her notebook and a pen. She was just about to open her phone when it rang.

Murphy closed the car door. He could hear Lynch's voice, but not what she was saying. He let his head fall back against the seat and closed his eyes.

The next thing he knew, Lynch was getting into the car. Murphy looked at his watch. Forty minutes had passed.

'Needing more sleep in your old age?' she asked with a smile on her face.

'Just remember who you're talking to,' said Murphy, also smiling. 'You'll be a sergeant for a long time if you talk to inspectors like that.'

'Not when you hear what I've found out,' said Lynch, starting the car.

Murphy waited for her to continue.

'The call was from my uncle,' she said. 'He asked around at Trinity College. It's been a few years since Geraldine Keane was a student there. Nobody remembers much about her – except for one thing. She was going out with another law student and, just before she left the college, they broke up very publicly.'

'How do you mean?' asked Murphy.

'A real fight – shouting, screaming, hitting each other – on the street right outside the main entrance to the college. Some other law students had to pull them away from each other.'

'Did you get her boyfriend's name?' asked Murphy.

'Michael Sullivan,' said Lynch as she pulled the car out into the traffic.

'What!' Murphy shook his head. 'Keane going out with someone like Sullivan. I can't see that at all.'

'Then I called the credit card company,' Lynch went on.

'And?' asked Murphy.

'This was not the first time flowers have been bought with that card.'

Murphy looked at Lynch.

'Over the last month, about once every two or three days, flowers have been bought from different flower shops across the city. I rang some of the shops and the flowers have all been sent to the same address,' continued Lynch.

'Orla Quinn's?' asked Murphy.

'Right,' said Lynch.

'And whose card is it?' asked Murphy.

'You tell me,' said Lynch still smiling.

Murphy got the name right first time.

'And that's where you're taking us?' asked Murphy.

'Of course,' replied Lynch.

Chapter 12 *There was a gun in his hand*

Geraldine Keane pushed angrily on the doorbell next to the red front door. No one answered. She pushed again. It was a long time since she had been to Michael Sullivan's house. It was just around the corner from Merrion Square and had belonged to Sullivan's parents. When they had died, he had moved in. Well, it was a nice part of town, thought Keane, and Sullivan was probably the richest person she'd ever known.

Still no one answered the door. Keane pushed the doorbell again and kept her finger on it. The bell rang and rang. Suddenly the door was thrown open. Sullivan stood there in jeans and an old T-shirt, looking tired.

'What ...?' he began, but then he saw who it was. 'You!' he said, taking half a step back. 'What are you doing here?'

Keane walked forwards, put a hand on his chest and pushed him back into the house.

'What do you think I'm doing here? You rat!'

She pushed him once more, leaving the door open behind her. Sullivan stepped back again, towards the kitchen.

'You used me,' said Keane, her voice cold and hard. 'You used me and then you threw me to one side.'

She pushed him into the kitchen, her eyes angry, a touch of red on each cheek.

'What are you talking about?' asked Sullivan. His hands were up in front of him, trying to keep her away.

'We agreed,' said Keane. 'I spent the night with you. And you promised to talk to the police – to make them believe I had nothing to do with the drug company break-in.'

'We didn't agree that,' said Sullivan quickly. 'I didn't promise anything.' But there was worry in his voice. 'I'm a lawyer,' he said. 'I couldn't agree to that. We just slept together like in the old days.'

Keane looked to her left. There was a bread knife next to the cooker. It was just what she needed. Promises were promises, and Sullivan needed to realise it was important to keep them. She picked up the knife and held it towards him.

'Geraldine!' said Sullivan. 'What are you doing?'

'You gave the papers to someone else, didn't you?' said Keane.

'Yes,' replied Sullivan. His back was now against the kitchen cupboards.

'That's a pity,' said Keane. 'A great pity – because I was really hoping you would keep your promise.'

'I couldn't,' said Sullivan quickly. 'I mean, I couldn't help you. The police could easily find out that we used to be lovers. Then I'd have been in real trouble.' Suddenly his eyes opened wide. 'My God!' he said. 'Orla Quinn.' He looked at the knife in Geraldine's hand. 'You ...' He didn't finish the sentence.

Geraldine took a step towards him.

* * *

George Keegan rode quickly into Merrion Square. He passed the house where the famous Irish writer Oscar Wilde once lived. Minutes later he stopped his motorbike outside Michael Sullivan's house. The front door was open.

That was strange. George jumped off the bike, and walked quickly towards the house.

There were voices coming from the kitchen at the back of the house. Loud voices.

Once he got inside, George walked more slowly, trying to discover what was happening. Just outside the kitchen door he stopped. He looked carefully round the door into the room. Michael Sullivan was standing, face towards the door, with his back against the kitchen cupboards. Geraldine Keane was moving towards Sullivan holding a bread knife in front of her. What was Geraldine Keane doing here? George didn't stop to think. He took three steps into the room and took Keane's arm in both his hands. He pushed her arm hard down onto the back of a wooden chair standing next to her.

Keane cried out and fell to the floor, dropping the knife. George pushed it away with his foot into the corner of the room.

'Thank God you're here,' said Sullivan, coming towards George. 'That woman wanted to kill me. I think she killed Orla.'

'Stay there, Michael,' said George. 'I have some questions for you.'

'What?' There was surprise in Sullivan's voice. 'This woman was trying to kill me. With a knife. That's what happened to Orla.'

'I had nothing to do with that,' said Keane, still on the floor. 'And he knows it. He used me. He promised . . .'

'Shut up!' said George. 'Shut up, both of you!'

There was quiet in the room for a moment. Keane and Sullivan kept their eyes on George.

'Michael,' said George. 'I've just got two questions for you.'

Sullivan looked at George and nodded.

'First,' said George, 'how did you know that Orla and I had been going out for just three weeks?'

'What?' asked Sullivan. 'What do you mean?' He looked as though he couldn't believe the question.

'Three weeks,' repeated George. 'Why were you so sure?'

'You told me earlier,' answered Sullivan. 'You said you'd only been going out together for three weeks.'

'No, I didn't,' replied George. 'I said we hadn't been going out for very long.'

'Oh! Come on, George,' said Sullivan. 'What's all this about? Three weeks. Not very long. It's all the same thing. What are you trying to say?'

'Question two,' said George. 'How did you know about Orla's window boxes?'

Sullivan just looked at George, his mouth open a little.

'Well?' said George. 'Tell me. How did you know that Orla's flat had window boxes? We only put them up last weekend – me and her. How did you know they were there?'

'She told me about them.'

'No, she didn't,' said George, his voice rising angrily. 'She didn't tell anyone because she and I did it together, and because we weren't telling anyone about "us".'

Sullivan moved uncomfortably from one foot to another.

'You know about the window boxes,' continued George, 'because you've been watching her flat, haven't you?'

Sullivan said nothing. His tongue moved over his lips as if his mouth was dry. He started moving around, taking short steps up and down the end of the kitchen.

'You don't understand, George. You don't know what you're talking about.'

Keane stayed on the floor, her eyes moving from one man to the other. She looked too afraid to get up.

'And about those flowers . . .' began George.

Sullivan had moved all the way across the kitchen. He was now near a long cupboard in the far corner of the room. Suddenly he turned, threw open the cupboard door and reached inside. He turned back quickly before George or Keane had time to move. There was a gun in his hand.

'Don't move,' Sullivan said. He looked at George. 'You think you know it all, don't you? Well, if you and Orla Quinn were so close, such good friends, lovers even, perhaps it's time you joined her.'

Chapter 13   *The madness of life and love and death*

Lynch drove round Merrion Square and then up towards Sullivan's house. There were no cars on either side of the street, just a motorbike right outside his house. Lynch stopped behind it. She and Murphy got out and walked towards Sullivan's front door. It was open. They looked at each other.

'I don't like the look of this,' said Murphy, taking out his phone. 'Let's get a few more people here.'

He made a quick call to the Pearse Street police station, and then he and Lynch entered the house. Slowly and carefully. There were voices coming from the back – Sullivan's and Keegan's.

Murphy was right by the kitchen door when he heard Sullivan's words, '... if you and Orla Quinn were so close, such good friends, lovers even, perhaps it's time you joined her.' He realised what was about to happen and spoke softly, but loudly enough for Sullivan to hear.

'Don't do anything stupid, Sullivan,' he said.

The kitchen went quiet. The only thing Murphy could hear was the low sound of traffic passing the end of the street outside.

'Listen to me, Sullivan,' said Murphy. 'I'm coming in. Alone. I haven't got a gun.'

'Where's your sergeant, Inspector?' asked Sullivan. 'You people always work in twos. Bring her in as well.'

Murphy looked at Lynch and she nodded at him.

'OK, OK,' said Murphy. 'We're both coming in. Neither of us has a gun and we're coming in slowly.'

Sullivan said nothing.

Slowly Murphy stepped into the kitchen. Lynch followed. Murphy looked round the room. Sullivan was standing with his back against the cupboard in the far corner of the room. He had a gun in his hand. Keane was sitting on the floor, holding her arm. Keegan was standing near Keane.

'We know about the flowers,' said Murphy, looking at Sullivan. He kept his voice light and soft. 'You sent some to Orla Quinn every two or three days from different flower shops. We found out from your credit card.'

'You sick man,' said George angrily.

Sullivan moved the gun quickly towards George.

'Shut up, Keegan,' said Murphy, his voice hard.

'Did she know the flowers were from you?' Murphy asked.

'Of course not,' replied Sullivan. 'I was going to tell her later – when we became a couple.'

'But then she got together with George Keegan,' continued Murphy.

'Why didn't you tell her how you felt?' asked Lynch.

'I asked her out once, but she laughed. She said she might go out with me another time. Maybe. I couldn't tell her how I felt. I didn't want her to laugh at me again. She was just so ...'

Sullivan didn't finish. His gun had started to move down towards the floor as though he was lost in thought. But

61

suddenly he realised what was happening and pulled the gun back up towards George.

'I'd never felt like that about anyone before,' Sullivan added.

Keane gave a short angry laugh. 'You certainly hadn't,' she said. 'You never had any feelings that I can remember.'

Sullivan moved the gun down towards Keane, fire in his eyes.

'How would you know anything about feelings for people?' Sullivan's voice was hard. 'You care more about animals than people.'

'OK, OK.' Murphy put his hands out in front of him. 'Everyone just keep quiet. Listen to me, Mr Sullivan. There are more police on their way here. I'm going to tell you what I think. After that I'd like you to put the gun down. Then we'll all go down to the police station and talk about it. OK?'

Sullivan brought the gun back towards Murphy.

'You left the bar the other night just after Keegan and Ms Quinn,' Murphy went on. 'You followed them to Keegan's flat. As they were opening the door, you used chloroform on Keegan. You probably told Ms Quinn it was some kind of joke. That kept her quiet for just long enough. Then you took out a knife and killed her, and made sure there was a lot of blood in the flat. You put the knife and a piece of her dress down the back of the sofa. How am I doing so far?'

Sullivan looked straight at Murphy but said nothing.

'Why did you do all this?' asked Murphy. 'Because you were madly in love with Ms Quinn, but she wasn't interested. And then, even worse, she started going out with Mr Keegan. So she dies and Keegan goes to prison. You kill two birds with one stone, as they say. Very clever.'

Keane's hand had gone to her mouth and her eyes were open wide. She looked as if she couldn't believe what she was hearing.

'Then you took her body, threw it in the river and came back here,' continued Murphy. 'Forensics are very good these days. You're a lawyer – you know that. What do you think we'll find here?' He looked round the room. 'Her blood on your clothes? On your shoes? Blood in your car? I'm sure you used your car to get the body to the river. You didn't just put her over your shoulder and walk there.'

There was a strange look on Sullivan's face. Lynch put her hand on Murphy's arm.

'Don't be too hard on him,' she whispered – making sure that Murphy could hear but no one else.

'What are forensics going to find, Mr Sullivan?' Murphy asked quietly.

He reached out a hand.

'Come on,' he said. 'Give me the gun. Let's end this.'

Sullivan didn't move. From the front of the house came noises. There was the sound of car doors opening and closing, voices, footsteps.

'Yes,' said Sullivan. 'Let's end it.'

Then quickly, before anyone could move, he put the gun in his mouth. There was a loud noise. Blood and bits of brain flew over the front of the cupboards behind Sullivan. Keane screamed and put her hands over her eyes. George turned away. Murphy and Lynch ran towards Sullivan's body as it fell to the floor.

As Murphy picked up the gun in his handkerchief, Lynch felt the side of Sullivan's neck. She looked up at Murphy and shook her head.

Forty minutes later, Murphy and Lynch were back in the car. Some officers had taken Keane and George Keegan to the Pearse Street police station to answer questions about what had happened. An ambulance had taken Sullivan's body away. Forensics were still in the house.

Lynch started the car and drove back through Merrion Square. As they passed Oscar Wilde's house, Murphy spoke.

'Do you like Oscar Wilde?' he asked.

'I prefer Yeats,' she said, naming another Irish writer. He had lived on the other side of the square. Then she repeated a couple of lines from something Yeats had written:

A pity beyond all telling
Is hid in the heart of love

Murphy smiled a little and put his head back against the seat. It was good that someone could explain the madness of life and love and death.